W9-AEP-596

WITHDRAWN

Horses As I See Them

Horses As I See Them

pictures by Ugo Mochi   text by Dorcas MacClintock

Charles Scribner's Sons   New York

Library of Congress Cataloging in Publication Data
MacClintock, Dorcas.
Horses as I see them.
1. Horses—History. 2. Horse breeds.
3. Horses—Pictorial works. 4. Shadow-pictures
I. Mochi, Ugo, 1889- II. Title.
SF285.M1527   636.1'009   78-31778   ISBN 0-684-16116-8
Permission to reprint pictures by Ugo Mochi on pages 36 and 38
from *Theodore Roosevelt's America*, Farida A. Wiley, ed.,
granted by The Devin-Adair Co., Old Greenwich, Conn. 06870.
Copyright © 1955 by The Devin-Adair Company.

To

EDNA MOCHI

with love and gratitude,

and to my father

JAMES T. EASON

for sharing my interest in horses

D. M.

Contents

1 / Horses in Outline /1

2 / Horses in Hand and in Motion /6

3 / Horses of Long Ago /12

Przewalski Horse/**12**

The Tarpan/**14**

4 / Horses and Man /16

5 / Breeds of Horses /22

6 / The Gentle Giants /27

The Percheron/**27**

The Clydesdale/**28**

The Suffolk/**28**

The Belgian/**30**

The Shire/**30**

The Breton/**30**

The Boulonnais/**31**

7 / Horses in the Americas /32

Out West/**33**

In the East/**41**

South America/**42**

8 / Horses under Saddle /45

On the Flat/**45**

Polo/**45**

Thoroughbreds and Racing/**47**

The American Quarter Horse/**50**

The Morgan Horse/**51**

The Saddlebreds/**52**

The Tennessee Walking Horse/**59**

Over Fences/**61**

Hunters/**61**

Jumpers/**63**

Show Jumping and Eventing/**65**

9 / Horses in Harness /69

The Fine Harness Horse/**69**

The Roadster/**70**

The Heavy Harness Horse/**71**

The Hackney Pony/**72**

Coaches and Carriages/**74**

Horses Bred for Harness/**77**

Trotting Horses/**80**

The Standardbred/**81**

The Orlov/**83**

10 / The Sprites /84

The Welsh Pony/**85**

The Dartmoor Pony/**86**

The Exmoor Pony/**86**

The New Forest Pony/**87**

The Connemara Pony/**88**

Horses have a special grace. Curves of neck and body, always balanced and beautiful, are influenced by mood. When horses stand together under a pasture shade tree, heads low and weight shifting from one hind leg to the other, their contours are passive. Suddenly heads go up, ears prick, and nostrils flare. Body contours suggest vigor and strength. The horses are alert, ready to turn and canter off—or, with a nicker of recognition, trot forward to nuzzle a pocket for grain.

Being creatures of grace and charm, horses have inspired artists for hundreds, even thousands of years. Long before horses were tamed, early hunters stalked their herds and ate their meat. These prehistoric peoples covered the walls of their caves with energetic likenesses of horses. Through 5,000 years of civilization, artists have continued to express their admiration of horses in painting and sculpture.

As a small boy during the 1890s Ugo Mochi admired horses, all kinds of horses. He made drawings and paper cutouts of the horses and carriages he saw on the streets of Florence and the cart horses that worked in the Italian countryside. He liked to go with his mother to the Bargello, the national museum in Florence. There he gazed in wonder at a cast of the *Gattamelata,* a famous equestrian statue by the Renaissance sculptor Donatello. Gattamelata, or "Cunning Cat," was the nickname of Erasmo da Narni, a general in command of the Venetian land forces during the 1400s. But it was the massive bronze horse, not his rider, that delighted Ugo Mochi. When he was ten, a small clay model he had made of Gattamelata's horse gained him admittance to the Academy of Fine Arts in Florence.

Ugo Mochi went on to study in Berlin under the animal sculptor August Gaul and the painter Paul Mayerheim. Although he worked much of the time in clay, he continued to cut animals from black paper. Often, as he worked, his studio companion was a black-and-white, or harlequin, Great Dane. After the success of a one-man show in London, the artist decided to concentrate on shadow outline. From then on Ugo Mochi worked in black on white.

Sculptural outline, among the oldest of art forms, traces back to prehistoric monochrome rock paintings in Europe and Africa. It finds expression in the black figures that decorate red vases made in Greece more than 2,000 years ago. This simple and direct art form becomes most exacting when the artist seeks to combine design, action, and form.

Form expressed in outline, unaffected by color or light, creates an immediate and dynamic three-dimensional impression. As Ugo Mochi says, "the unchanging thing which makes the appearance of every animal different from every other is its shape." The artist's preoccupation with the form of horses, in all their variety of sizes and shapes, rather than the colors or patterns which obscure their body outlines, give his cutouts a sculptural quality. It also leaves no room for error of interpretation, for an incorrect body line or a misplaced limb would stand out, black on white.

The materials of sculptural outline are heavy black paper and a small lithographer's knife. The artist makes a rough sketch and places it over black paper on a glass-topped surface. Then his skilled hand deftly guides the pencil-shaped knife as it cuts the horse in outline.

Without using color or shading, Ugo Mochi suggests both mood and motion. His black paper horses are more lively and spirited than those of most artists who work with brushes, palette, and pigments. To attain perspective, he often foreshortens his horses, as he has done with the lumbering dray team. Yet

2

the outline of their powerful shapes is so accurate that the viewer has no difficulty filling in details.

When I first met this artist he was at work on the illustrations for *Hoofed Mammals of the World,* a book written by T. Donald Carter of the American Museum of Natural History. Learning of my interest in horses, he drew from his pocket a horse and buggy, a cutout so small that it could just be seen between his fingertips. The detail was unbelievable. The buggy was a doctor's phaeton, the kind of vehicle once used by country doctors on their calls. The doctor himself sat on the seat. He had a loose hold on the driving reins as his blinkered horse trotted along. From this moment on I was under the spell of Ugo Mochi's horses.

Each cutout is one piece: horse, rider, fence, clouds—all are cut from a single sheet of paper. Cart horses strain to pull a heavy load, hunters and jumpers are supple in their movements, trotters go to the wire in close formation, polo ponies gallop after the ball, and giant draft horses stand in profile. These and more are horses as Ugo Mochi sees them.

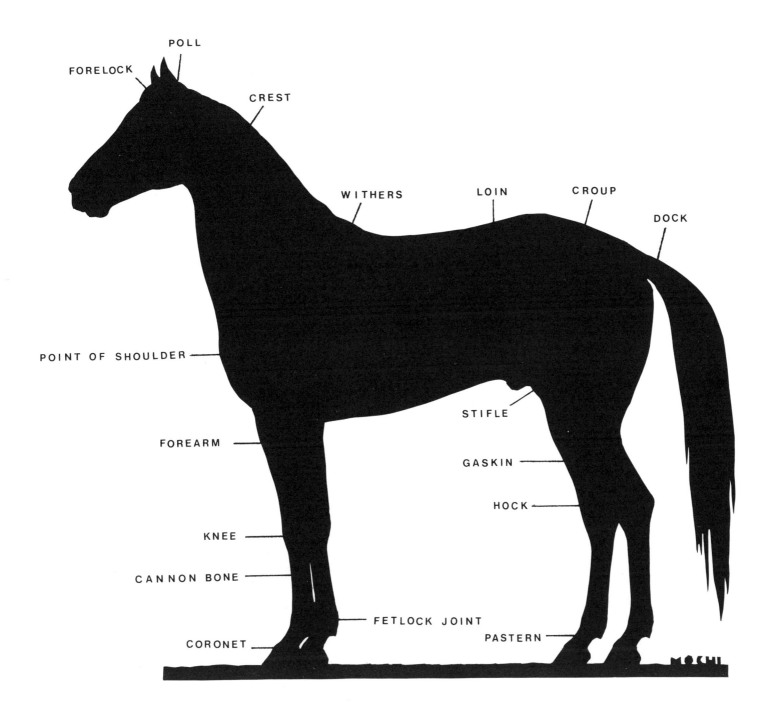

POLL

FORELOCK

CREST

WITHERS   LOIN   CROUP

DOCK

POINT OF SHOULDER

STIFLE

FOREARM

GASKIN

HOCK

KNEE

CANNON BONE

FETLOCK JOINT   PASTERN

CORONET

MOCHI

With the eye of a horseman, Ugo Mochi views each subject point by point. His feeling for horses gives him a sure hand in portraying the gestures that give life and motion to each animal, whether it is a saddlebred in the show ring, a jumper clearing an oxer, a bronco bucking to unseat its rider, or a wild stallion guarding his mares.

Ugo Mochi also knows about tack—bridles, saddles, harnesses, halters, and lead shanks. While a snaffle bit is used on many hunters, this mare, with side saddle just removed, requires a full or double bridle, which suggests she is strong-going. A saddlebred is always ridden in full bridle, often one that has a

shiny, bright-colored browband. The long-shanked curb bit induces flexion at the poll (the point between a horse's ears). The snaffle, or bridoon, the upper bit in the mouth, is used to maintain high head carriage.

As for saddles, a forward seat or jumping saddle, usually with contoured flaps that allow close contact of rider's legs to horse's body, is preferred by hunt-seat riders. The saddlebred is ridden with a flat saddle that has a cut-back pommel and straight flaps, a design that shows off the horse's forehand (front end or shoulders) and places the rider well back in the saddle.

The Hackney horse about to be backed between the shafts of a two-wheeled tilbury wears a light harness that includes a check rein to keep its head high. A crupper runs from harness pad to tail. Its bridle is fitted with a Liverpool driving bit and blinkers that cut off vision to the side and from behind, thus reducing the horse's tendency to shy at strange objects along the road.

Work horses wear heavy padded leather collars into which wooden hames are fitted. When traces are attached to the hames, the collars absorb the hauling weight and prevent sore shoulders. Singly or in teams, the big horses are willing workers as long as they receive consideration and good care.

Ugo Mochi understands horses in motion and the sequence of hoof-fall in their three natural gaits: walk, trot or pace, and gallop. The walk is a smooth, four-beat movement that is comfortable to the rider. Trotting is a two-beat gait. Legs move in diagonal pairs, left fore and right hind together, then right

fore and left hind. Between beats, for a brief instant that occurs twice during each stride, all four hoofs are off the ground. Horses that pace also travel in two-beat cadence, but lateral leg pairs (legs on the same side) move together. Although pacing occurs naturally in some harness racers, most horses must be trained to pace. At top speed, horses gallop. There is a three-beat cadence with broken rhythm: beat, pause, beat, quick double beat, beat, pause. . . . During the single pause in each stride, all four hoofs are off the ground for a fleeting moment. An extended gallop may have a four-beat hoof-fall.

The canter is a slow, in-hand or collected gallop that has a pleasing swing and rhythm. The motion is backward and forward rather than up and down (as in the trot). The gait is said to have originated in the Middle Ages when pilgrims, celebrated by the English poet Geoffrey Chaucer, on their way to

Thomas à Becket's cathedral, favored this ground-covering yet not tiring way of going. In time, the so-called Canterbury gallop was shortened to "canter."

Like the gallop, the three-beat canter (with four beats sounding when the gait is much slowed and high action is accentuated) is led by the foreleg on one side or the other. Leads are important to the horse's balance. In the show ring a horse should canter on the inside lead, its inside foreleg reaching out farther than the other foreleg. Running free, horses switch easily from one lead to the other. Lead change occurs during the brief moment of suspension. To get around the tight turns of a course, show jumpers execute smooth flying changes (shifts of lead at the canter or gallop). A sharp turn on the wrong or outside lead risks a fall, always a shaking experience for horse as well as rider.

Trained gaits such as the rack and slow gait of the Five-gaited Saddle Horse and the swinging, loose-jointed, running walk of the Tennessee Walking Horse are variations in speed and style of the horse's three natural gaits.

3 / Horses of Long Ago

Among the animal figures painted on the dark walls and ceilings of caves in southern France and northern Spain are wild horses, descendants of the pony-size wild horses that roamed over much of Eurasia during the Pleistocene, the geological epoch that began two million years ago. Painted by cave artist–hunters some 15,000 years ago, these lifelike horses have heavy, often bearded heads, thick necks, bristly upright manes, back stripes, and mealy-colored noses. Many of them look like the Przewalski horse (Asiatic wild horse) of today; others resemble the extinct tarpan (European wild horse).

PRZEWALSKI HORSE

Never domesticated, this true wild horse, the last of its kind, stands about 13.2 hands high. Dun or sandy bay, it has a dark brown or black 6-inch mane that stands up stiffly like a brush, a large head, thick neck, and straight back. It has no forelock. Down its back, from the mane to the long black hairs of the tail, runs a dark stripe. Short, light-colored hairs cover the upper third of the tail. Dark leg markings vary from fetlock bands to stockings that reach to knee and hock. Occasionally, zebralike bands mark the upper forelegs.

Przewalski horses, like their relatives the zebras and the wild asses, undergo a yearly molt of mane and tail. Domestic horses shed their mane and tail hairs a few at a time, year round. It is the annual molt that maintains the hogged-mane and pulled-tail appearance of Przewalski horses.

Low withers and gentle slope of croup give the Przewalski horse a compact body profile. Head on, it has a ponylike expression, with black-edged ears tipped inward, eyes that are prominent, dark, and bright, and a muzzle that is neatly chiseled. Mealy color marks the muzzle and rings the eyes.

Przewalski horses were unknown until a century ago, when the Russian explorer Nikolai Mikhailovitch Przewalski acquired the skin and skull of a wild horse, shot by native hunters in the Mongolian desert, and presented them to the Museum of the Imperial Academy of Sciences in St. Petersburg (now the

PRZEWALSKI

Zoological Institute of the Soviet Academy of Sciences in Leningrad). The curator of the museum carefully compared the specimens with other equid material (all horses, as well as wild asses and zebras, belong to the family Equidae), and in 1881 he described a new species of horse. He named the species *Equus przewalskii* in honor of the explorer.

This discovery created a stir among zoologists, especially those who were animal collectors. In 1897, the Baron Friedrich von Falz-Fein, who owned a vast animal sanctuary-estate in the Ukraine, arranged with a Russian merchant for the capture of some young Przewalski horses. Two years later, four fillies arrived safely at Askania Nova, von Falz-Fein's estate. Between 1899 and 1904, a number of consignments of wild horses were made to Russia and Germany.

Listed as an endangered species in the Red Data Book of the International Union for Conservation of Nature and Natural Resources (the IUCN), the Przewalski horse probably has been exterminated in the wild, gone even from the bare and desolate desert region of southern Mongolia that was its last stronghold. No longer do small family bands, each consisting of a stallion and his mares with foals, wear trails over the sandy rock-strewn soil or graze tussock grasses and browse on woody shrubs in the Takhin Shara Nuru, or "Mountain of the Yellow Horses."

Fortunately, Przewalski horses breed well in captivity. Zoos in Europe and the United States are dedicated to preserving herds of these last wild horses, nearly all of them descended from twenty-eight horses shipped in 1901 to the German animal dealer Carl Hagenbeck. In 1977, forty-nine Przewalski foals were born, six of them in the United States, where the Catskill Game Farm, the New York Zoological Park, the San Diego Zoo, and the Memphis Zoo have breeding herds. The 1978 Stud Book, edited by Dr. Jiří Volf of the Prague Zoological Garden, lists 299 living Przewalski horses.

THE TARPAN

Now extinct, the grayish or mouse-dun tarpan was the wild horse of Europe, described from four specimens collected in a remote region of the Ukraine in

1769 by the German naturalist Samuel Gottlieb Gmelin. Tarpan herds grazed the steppes of southern Russia until the mid-1800s.

Lighter in build than its Asiatic counterpart, *Equus przewalskii gmelini* was dish-faced and had a dark reddish-brown mane and tail, a wide spinal stripe, and black leg markings that extended well above knee and hock. Usually the brushy mane grew long enough to topple onto one or both sides of its neck. In winter the tarpan's light-gray coat turned almost white.

Stallions frequently abducted domestic mares into their herds. Because of this tendency, the tarpan's status as a true wild horse has been called into question. The last full-blooded wild tarpan may have been a mare that grazed in the company of domestic horses, occasionally following them into paddock and stable, until her death in 1880.

During the early 1930s in Germany, two brothers began attempts to re-create the tarpan by back-breeding. Heinz Heck at the Hellabrunn Zoo in Munich and Lutz Heck at the Berlin zoo selected for primitive tarpanlike traits among domestic breeds. They crossed Icelandic ponies and koniks (small Polish horses) with a Przewalski stallion. Successive cross-breedings produced a light-built, mouse-dun or gray pony whose characteristics fitted the tarpan descriptions of Gmelin and others. These back-bred tarpans, now maintaining their type, can be seen at the Catskill Game Farm in New York State (where Dr. Heinz Heck, son and nephew of the tarpan breeders, is director) and at the Munich zoo.

TARPAN

4 / Horses and Man

Ancient nomadic tribes of central Asia were the first to domesticate horses some 5,000 years ago. Although the Scythians and other tribes left no records, it is probable that they introduced horses into the Near East and China. Historical records of domestic horses extend back to at least 2000 B.C. in Mesopotamia, an ancient country between the Tigris and Euphrates rivers. By that time, pony-size horses had been obtained by trading with nomads from the north.

Horses soon proved themselves superior to the onagers (horselike Asiatic wild asses) and oxen already in use. Stronger and swifter than the onager, the horse was ideal for pulling chariots. By 1700 B.C., light, spoke-wheeled chariots replaced the ponderous, rumbling designs pulled by two or four onagers. Among the most dashing horsemen of the ancient world were the Thracians, who fashioned chariot ornaments and bridle decorations of gold and silver and lived a life of battles and banditry on horseback. Their conquests aided the spread of horses.

The condition of horses improved when their human masters began to care for them, providing shelter and feed. Within a few generations, their size increased. The horse, *Equus caballus,* had begun its important role in the history of human progress, a role it would play first in the Old World and later on in the New World.

It is not known exactly when people began to use horses for riding. The earliest hint is a wooden figure of a man on a horse from an Egyptian tomb of about 1350 B.C. The man rides in donkey-seat position, so called because a donkey has a sharp backbone which can be avoided by sitting far back, as does this young falconer on a horse. The position also takes up more of the rider's leg, an advantage on a small mount.

On horseback men felt themselves invincible and so horses became all-important in war. A vivid description of the horse in battle comes from the Book of Job, written about 500 B.C.: "The glory of his nostrils is terrible. He paweth in the valley, and rejoiceth in his strength. He goeth on to meet the armed men. He swalloweth the ground with fierceness and rage."

The Persians had especially fine horses. In 490 B.C., when the Persian army invaded Greece, the superiority of their horse troops was so apparent that the commander of the Greek forces sent out only his foot soldiers.

In Egypt and much of the region between the Caspian Sea and the Sahara, the Saluki, a greyhoundlike dog with silky hair that hangs from its ears, legs, and long, graceful tail, was used for chasing gazelles, jackals, and hares. Well-muscled shoulders and thighs and arched loins suggest the speed of this gazehound, which pursues its prey by sight rather than smell. The breed is so old that its likeness (and sometimes its remains, for the Saluki was the royal dog of Egypt) is found in tombs constructed along the Upper Nile in 2100 B.C. On occasion the pharaoh himself rode to the chase with a hawk on his wrist and one or more Salukis on leash.

The Greeks are renowned for their horses in art, small statues in bronze and marble and paintings on vases and plates. The lively horses of the Parthenon with their youthful bareback riders form a continuous band of relief sculpture. Carved into the frieze nearly 2,500 years ago, the procession honors the goddess Athena, whose temple stands on the Acropolis in Athens.

During the third century B.C., Alexander the Great rode his legendary charger, Bucephalus. The spirited black stallion carried his rider to victory after victory until much of Asia was under Greek rule.

From Greek mythology comes the story of Pegasus, the winged horse

whose ability to fly made his rider, Bellerophon, a dreaded warrior. When Bellerophon guided Pegasus toward heaven, he infuriated the god Zeus, who retaliated by sending a fly to sting the horse. Poor Bellerophon was unseated and fell to earth. Pegasus, as is well known, flew on to become a constellation.

On the plains of Olympia, four-horse chariot races were exciting spectacles. Today's Olympic Games trace back to these ancient competitions. Chariot racing was also popular in Rome, where spectators filled the hippodromes to watch chariot teams of two, three, or four horses compete. Often the chariot drivers became warriors, causing their chariots to collide. Horses were injured and charioteers hurtled through the air.

Horses figured importantly in the formation of the Chinese Empire, from the time of the Han Dynasty (202 B.C.–A.D. 220). Chinese artists depicted in pottery and paintings a big horse, with exaggerated chest and croup, a tapirlike nose, and rather slim legs. The Chinese were proud of these pompous, 16-hands-high steeds, which they had imported from Bactria, an ancient Greek empire in central Asia. In fact, at one time they imported so many horses that the people of Bactria refused to allow any more out of the country, and a Bactrian war ensued. The Chinese won and demanded delivery of 100 of the finest Bactrian horses for breeding purposes, as well as some 300 more horses for general use.

During the T'ang Dynasty (A.D. 618–907), these Bactrian horses were brilliantly portrayed. Mold-cast of colored clay with hollow cores, T'ang horses range in height from 5 inches to 2½ feet. Some stand four square, others prance. Their features were sensitively modeled, and often the mouth was open to suggest spirited impatience. Most of them were painted in browns and amber with color splashed on manes and trappings. Less often a blue glaze was used.

These glazed pottery horses were funerary figures. Placed in the tomb of a high-ranking official, the clay horses replaced the real horses which earlier Chinese custom demanded be slain and buried with their deceased masters. Symbolically these heavenly horses, as they are sometimes called, carried their riders' souls to heaven.

The Arabs had fleet horses which they prized. Followers of the prophet Muhammad, mounted on superb horses, conquered tribe after tribe in the sixth century. They rode into Spain, where their small Arab- and Barb-type horses outmaneuvered the heavy Spanish horses with their armor-clad riders. In France, the Muslims encountered heavily armored warriors on huge black Flemish Horses. Finally, at the Battle of Tours in the year 732, the invaders met defeat.

5 / Breeds of Horses

SHETLAND   SHIRE

From the wild horses that roamed Eurasia during the Pleistocene epoch are derived all the breeds of horses, from ponderous Shire to diminutive Shetland pony.

Although some of the pony breeds are more closely related to the ancestral wild horses, the breeds of horses developed from two strains: the small, swift, Arab and Barb types and the big, heavy Great Horse of the Middle Ages.

Perfection of conformation and balance characterize the true Arabian, the treasured horse of the nomadic Bedouin tribes. Bred for stamina and to withstand desert extremes of heat by day and cold by night, the Arabian excels in endurance and intelligence as well as beauty.

The Arabian is small, 14 to 15 hands being preferred height. But it is a strong horse. Its back is short and its hoofs are tough. The head is short and refined, with a distinctly dished profile. The *jibbah,* or broad bulging forehead, is unique to the breed. The neck is slim and arched, the chest large and powerful. High withers slope onto a back that has one less lumbar vertebra than other horses have. The croup forms an almost straight line, and the tail is carried like a banner in the wind.

The typical light riding horse of the Barbary States of Algeria and Morocco in northwest Africa, the Barb was less spirited and less refined than the

ARABIAN

Arabian. But it showed speed and endurance that suited it for racing and light cavalry use. Knee action characterized the Barb's way of going, a tendency that shows up in trotting horses and light harness breeds as well as in the Andalusian horses whose descendants repopulated the Americas.

During the Middle Ages, war was a way of life. As heavier and more cumbersome armor replaced breastplate and helmet in jousting tournaments and in battle, the need arose for big, strong horses. From the eleventh to the fourteenth century, Crusaders rode into battle on giant steeds as they sought to wrest the Holy Land from the Muslims. By the fifteenth century, a knight encased in a suit of jointed plate armor weighed as much as 400 pounds and had to be hoisted onto his horse by block and tackle. His charger (for by this time the charge had replaced cavalry maneuvers that were too intricate for the big horses) also carried its own protective armor of jointed steel plates and skirting. Medieval tapestries and paintings often show horses and riders completely obscured by armor and colorful trappings.

There were various strains of these armor-carrying Great Horses. The earliest distinct type was the Flemish Horse, presumably bred from *Equus robustus,* a large and lumbering horse of prehistoric Europe. When the French obtained these horses, they developed the Norman Horse. Taken to England in 1066 by William the Conqueror, Norman Horses crossed with native horses to produce the Black Horse.

The medieval Great Horse is commemorated in Italy, where it became the model for such Renaissance artists as Leonardo da Vinci, Verrocchio, and Titian. Roman emperors, Marcus Aurelius in the Campidoglio Square on Rome's Capitoline Hill and Caligula in Naples, are astride horses that are heroic in size and substance. Military heroes, Gattamelata in Padua and Colleoni in Venice, also ride proud and powerful steeds.

The sculptor Donatello modeled Gattamelata's mount—the horse that so impressed Ugo Mochi as a child—with its head slightly turned. Its tail is neatly folded and tied to the bone. Bare-headed and imposing, the general is clad in the armor of Roman antiquity and sits straight-legged in the saddle. He reaches forward, truncheon in hand, as if to touch the great bronze horse's mane.

Centuries of cross-breeding hot-blooded horses (Arabian and Thoroughbred) with massive cold-blooded types (draft horses) have produced the mix-

BERBER   KOEHL

CRUSADERS HORSE   KOEHL

XV CENT.   KOEHL

ROMAN   KOEHL

tures of size, structure and temperament that are the breeds of horses, some 180 in all.

Environment also has played a part in the development of horse breeds. In Bashkiria, a region on the southern slopes of the Ural Mountains in Russia, horses with curly coats have long been used for transportation, clothing, meat, and milk. From mares' milk, the Bashkirs make a fermented drink called *kumiss*.

Originally, the curly horse of Bashkiria was sorrel with flaxen legs. Its coat is long and curly. In winter the hairs grow 4 to 6 inches long. Winter-coat patterns vary from crushed velvet to all-over waves to tight ringlets covering the entire body. Curls line the short, broad ears, and even the horse's eyelashes are curly. Oddly slanted eyes give the curly horse a sleepy expression. And, perhaps to limit the intake of cold air, its nostrils are unusually small.

Curly horses are also known in the western United States, where ranchers claim they do twice the work on half the feed of an ordinary cow horse. Just how the curly horse came to North America is unknown. Some claim these horses, first seen in the Pacific Northwest, made their way across the Bering Strait during the Pleistocene. A more likely explanation is that curly-coatedness appeared independently in different horse populations. The American Bashkir Curly Horse Registry lists the curlies in the United States and encourages their use in endurance trail riding, barrel racing, and other events.

CURLY HAIRED BREED from DASHKIR

From the Great Horse of the Middle Ages, bred for war, are descended the draft horses, gentle giants that weigh a ton or more and stand up to 20 hands high.

Bred for work on the farm, drafters tilled the land, their heads and necks low and their shoulders plunged deep into their collars. Some of the heavy horses were used in teams to pull the great jouncing coaches from town to town. Others were dray horses whose huge hoofs clip-clopped on city streets.

Although tractors and trucks gradually replaced these big horses during the early 1900s, some farmers were too fond of their loyal teams to give them up. Draft horses are still seen at state fairs where, groomed and braided, they are led into the ring, or shown in hand, and judged on conformation. Now and then, an eight-horse hitch is exhibited at a country fair. But it is the horse-drawing contests, where a weighted stone-boat is used to test pulling power, that brings out the largest number of these hard-working, good-tempered horses.

THE PERCHERON

This French draft horse, descended from the Norman Horse and Arab and Barb horses introduced by invading Muslims, is native to the Perche district of

Normandy. Graceful body proportions belie its massive strength. Unlike other draft breeds that have conspicuous Roman noses, the Percheron has a finely shaped, well-chiseled head. Its way of going is animated. And it is almost always gray or black. Two gray Arabian stallions, much used in Percheron breeding during the early 1800s, influenced both head shape and body color.

A smaller version was the 15.2-hands-high harness Percheron, a well-proportioned, powerfully muscled horse with stylish gaits. This was the coach horse of France that pulled the huge diligences (public stagecoaches) over rough roads. Teams of four, six, or eight traveled at such a jaunty pace (7 to 10 miles per hour) that their gray color, which made the diligences visible at night, was regarded as a safety factor.

THE CLYDESDALE

Muscular strength and agility combine in this drafter, bred during the 1700s in the Clyde River valley of southern Scotland. Bay or brown, sometimes black, the Clydesdale has a lot of white on face and legs, and generous white splashes often mark its underbelly and hindquarters. Heavily feathered lower legs add to the showiness of a Clydesdale jogged on a lead shank or trotting in an eight-horse hitch. Hocks set close together and well under the hindquarters contribute to the breed's animated action. Its flashy trot covers ground with a high, springy style.

Clydesdales were the favorite dray horses of city merchants who took pride in their matched teams that trotted along the cobbled streets.

THE SUFFOLK

This oldest of the draft breeds is named for the county of its origin. In spite of the fact that all Suffolks are chestnut, the breed traces back to the Black Horse. And in the pedigree of all Suffolks appears the Crisp Horse, a stallion owned by a Mr. Crisp of Ufford, England. Perhaps because of its chunky conformation and short legs, the Suffolk also goes by the name Suffolk Punch.

CLYDESDALE

A. MOCHI

Most Suffolks have flaxen manes and tails. White markings are frowned upon by breeders, although a star on the forehead is permissible. What this 16-hand drafter lacks in stature and flashiness it makes up for in its honest and willing nature and pulling power. The Suffolk habit of throwing its weight into the collar makes this noted puller the favorite of many British farmers.

THE BELGIAN

Short-backed and solidly built, the Belgian is the heaviest of the draft horses, weighing from 1,900 to 2,200 pounds or more. Massive body width gives it a paddling, rolling way of going. Most Belgians are blaze-faced chestnuts with flaxen manes and tails. A few are roans.

More often than not, it is a team of four or six huge Belgians, digging in with their forefeet and straining their powerful hindquarters, that wins the pulling contests at country fairs. These hard-working natives of Belgium, descendants of the Flemish Horse, acquired their strength from centuries of toiling in the deep soil of the Low Country.

THE SHIRE

Directly descended from the Black Horse of seventeenth- and eighteenth-century England is the towering, rangy Shire. First bred in Lincolnshire and Cambridgeshire, two counties in east-central England, it is the largest of all horses. Black, brown, or bay, a Shire usually has a star or stripe on its face and high white stockings on its heavily feathered legs.

THE BRETON

From the Brittany peninsula of northwestern France comes a hardy, compact, thickset 15.2-hand horse, usually gray, bay, or roan, that is used for general farm work. Known for its docility, the Breton has a gentle expression.

THE BOULONNAIS

Sixteen to 17 hands high, this massive horse of enormous weight, well-developed bone, and powerful muscles is named for the town of Boulogne in France. Its ancestry, like the Percheron's, includes some Arab blood. Black, bay, roan, or gray, Boulonnais horses were valued as fast-moving coach horses of remarkable endurance.

31

7 / Horses in the Americas

The North American continent was the center of horse evolution from the time of eohippus, a small browsing bush dweller that lived in the Eocene epoch fifty million years ago, until the appearance of *Equus* (the genus of all living horses, asses, and zebras) at the end of the Pliocene some three million years ago. During this long expanse of geological time, some equids migrated across the wide Alaska-Siberia land connection, and side branches evolved in Eurasia. But it was in North America that the main evolutionary line flourished.

Then, some 8,000 years ago, horses vanished from North America. Their disappearance was part of a large-scale extinction that involved 70 percent of the large mammals, including woolly mammoths, mastodons, camels, and ground sloths. This wave of death began in the northwest and swept southeastward eventually across the Isthmus of Panama and into South America.

The probable cause of this extinction was a relative newcomer to North America—the human being. People had long hunted horses in Eurasia, and herds there were wary. But horses in North America were unacquainted with this new and relentless predator armed with throwing sticks and darts. As these prehistoric people pressed southward from the Bering Strait in ever-increasing numbers, hunting increased until finally horses were gone from North America.

Horses returned to the Americas with the Spaniards. Following Columbus's discovery of the New World in 1492, they brought horses into the West Indies, the base for their explorations in South America, Mexico, and Florida. In 1519 Hernando Cortés landed near Vera Cruz, Mexico, with sixteen horses.

At first the Aztec Indians were terrified by the spectacle of Cortés and his men on horseback. But they rallied to defeat the Spaniards and kill their horses. Then came more horses, mounts which the conquistadors rode to blaze a trail of blood and plunder across Mexico. The horses were Andalusians, bred from Barb stock, brought into that province in southern Spain during the Moorish invasion, and light Iberian horses. The Andalusians had the typical Barb head with somewhat convex facial profile. And they were sturdy, fast, and good-tempered.

In the wake of the conquistadors came merchants, missionaries, miners, and stockmen, all eager to exploit the new land. With them came thousands of cattle, sheep, and horses. Slowly the settlers moved northward, lured by vast grazing lands and rich silver mines.

Under the watchful eyes of mounted Spanish vaqueros or cowhands, Pueblo Indians taken as slaves tended the Spanish settlers' herds on foot. It was only a matter of time before some of the Indians learned to ride and galloped off into the surrounding mountains. Soon other Indian tribes began to raid horses from the settlers. In 1680, a Pueblo revolt drove out the Spanish and scattered their range stock. This event gave impetus to a 100-year northward spread of horses through western North America. By barter, trade, and theft, horses were acquired by one Indian tribe after another.

OUT WEST

Horses made it possible for the Plains Indians to move with the great herds of buffalo and aided the pursuit and killing of the shaggy animals. With bare legs locked around the pony's barrel, an Indian could keep pace with a running buffalo and, letting the reins dangle, plunge a lance into its shoulder.

Often buffalo hunting involved collaboration. Stampeding a herd toward a cliff, the Indians swerved their ponies as the terrified buffaloes thundered

over the edge. The result was a supply of meat and warm robes that would last through the winter.

West of the Rocky Mountains, the Navajos and the Utes traded horses north to the Shoshonis, the Crows, and the Blackfeet. By 1710, horses had been acquired by the Nez Percé tribe, whose territory included lush high meadows for summer grazing and sheltered valleys for winter range. These salmon-fishing Indians became expert horse breeders. Unlike the Plains Indians, who always preferred to ride their best war ponies and buffalo-chasing horses and left the scruffy stallions to run with the mares, the Nez Percés selected the best of their horses for breeding. They culled their herds and traded off or gelded inferior colts. Wrote the explorer Meriwether Lewis in 1806: "Their horses appear to be of an excellent race; . . . eligantly [sic] formed, active and durable. . . . Some . . . are pided [pied] with large spots of white irregularly scattered and intermixed with the black, brown, bey [sic] or some other dark color. . . ." What

Captain Lewis saw, of course, were the spotted horses called Palouseys (for the Palouse River, or "Stream of the Green Meadows"), the Appaloosa horses. Known in China as far back as twenty centuries ago, these curiously spotted horses made their way, through wars and conquests, from Asia to Spain and eventually to Mexico and the Pacific Northwest.

Two hundred years after the Spanish settlers' arrival, herds of wild horses were scattered over half of North America. These were the mustangs, "the coyote duns, the smokies, the blues, the blue roans, the snip-nosed pintos, the flea-bitten grays and the black-skinned whites, the shining blacks and the rusty browns, the red roans, the toasted sorrels and the stockinged bays, the splotched appaloosas and the cream-maned palominos, and all the others in shadings of color as various as the hues that show and fade on the clouds at sunset," described by the historian J. Frank Dobie. A few mustangs, horses of exceptional looks and speed, became legends. One was the Pacing White

Stallion, or Ghost Horse of the Plains, said to have paced all the way from the Mexican mesa country to the Dakota Bad Lands. Around the campfires on his prairie tour in the 1830s, Washington Irving heard "anecdotes . . . of a famous gray horse which has ranged the prairies for six or seven years, setting at naught every attempt to catch him. They say he can pace . . . faster than the fleetest horse can run."

Mustangs played a vital role in the opening up of the West. They were rounded up and broken for use as cow ponies. Explorers, trappers, and traders used them for riding and for transporting gear and goods in pack trains that crossed the high plains. Ranchers used them for hunting as well as for herding stock. Mustangs also found their way into the Pony Express and the United States Cavalry.

Mustang comes from the Spanish word *mestengo,* or stray. Wild or half-wild mustangs off the range were called broncos. Bronc-busting was a tough job. Large ranches maintained their own bronc-buster, for each cow hand had at least eight cow ponies for his own use. On small ranches, bronc-busters found temporary employment. A horse that resisted the bronc-buster's harsh methods was termed an outlaw and often found its way into the rodeo.

Mustangs are no more. The wild horses of the West today are in fact animals that have escaped from ranch herds. Their blood is a mixture of mustang and other strains and their existence is contested by ranchers who protest their grazing rights.

Rodeos date from the days of open range when annual roundup time brought together cow hands from several ranches. In the first rodeo on record, held in 1869, cow hands from three Colorado ranches—the Hash Knife, the Camp Stool, and the Mill Iron—displayed their riding and roping skills. By the 1880s, the fencing of range lands put an end to these informal contests, and rodeos became organized events. Bareback riding, calf roping, steer wrestling (or bulldogging), saddle-bronc riding, and bull riding are the main events of a rodeo.

Calf roping requires a fast horse. The loop sails through the air and lands over the calf's neck. Releasing the coils of his rope as the horse slides on its hocks to a stop, the cow hand swings to the ground. With one hand on the line, he runs toward the calf. The horse moves about to keep the rope taut. The cow hand throws the calf, ties one foreleg and two hind legs with the piggin string he has carried clenched in his teeth. With a good roping horse, all this is done in fifteen seconds or less.

Saddle-bronc horses are the best of the bucking horses. In saddle-bronc riding, the contestant must spur his horse and keep one hand free while the other clings to the halter rope. If he loses a stirrup or "pulls leather" (grabs for the saddle), he is disqualifed. And he must stay aboard for ten bone-jarring seconds.

IN THE EAST

While most of the horses in the colonies along the Atlantic coast were brought from England by the settlers, horses of Spanish origin spread north from Florida, introducing some of the Andalusian blood that ran pure in the early horses of the West.

Perhaps the most celebrated horse of colonial times was Paul Revere's mount. On April 18, 1775, this horse carried the silversmith on his midnight ride from Boston to Concord to warn that British soldiers were coming. "Paul Revere's Ride" was recounted nearly a century later by the poet Henry Wadsworth Longfellow:

> . . . A hurry of hoofs in a village street,
> A shape in the moonlight, a bulk in the dark,
> And beneath, from the pebbles, in passing, a spark
> Struck out by a steed flying fearless and fleet;
> That was all! And yet, through the gloom and the light,
> The fate of a nation was riding that night;
> And the spark struck out by that steed, in his flight,
> Kindled the land into flame with its heat.

Soon horses were being bred for specific purposes. Five breeds are truly American: the Standardbred, the American Saddlebred, the American Quarter Horse, the Morgan Horse, and the Tennessee Walking Horse. All had their beginnings in the East.

SOUTH AMERICA

The horse breeds of South America, like the mustangs of the West, are descended from imported Spanish horses abandoned by fleeing settlers or strayed from ranches along the foothills of the Andes. Herds of these horses grazed and galloped free on the pampas, a harsh environment of prairie fires, dust storms, and cold. They were the ancestors of the South American breeds.

Gauchos, the cowboys of South America, are superb riders. With scarlet ponchos billowing in the wind, they gallop fearlessly over the rough pampas. They have a saying: *Despreciar el grande y ensillar el pequeño*—Reject the big and saddle the small. In other words, gauchos prefer small horses.

A favorite breed is the Criollo, a small (13.2 to 14.3 hands high), tough, and wiry horse. For working livestock on the pampas, the Criollo has no equal in ability or endurance. Criollos come in several colors, but back-lined horses, those with a dark stripe along the spine, are preferred. The head is short and pyramid-shaped, the withers are muscular, the back is straight and short loined, and the croup is large. The short-legged Criollo gallops with its hind legs moving well apart.

Pursuit of large, fast-running, flightless birds called rheas was once a pastime of the gauchos. Sometimes a gaucho on his Criollo tried to lasso the bird. More often *bolas,* two- or three-thonged leather slings weighted with stones, were used. Thrown skillfully, the bola wrapped around the fleeing rhea's legs, ending the chase.

Criollos are bright and active. The naturalist and novelist W. H. Hudson described the behavior of a gaucho's horse named Cristiano, loosely tied to a *palenque,* or hitching post: "A more restless horse I had never seen. His head was always raised as high as he could raise it—like an ostrich, the gauchos would say—his gaze fixed excitedly on some far object; then presently he would reel round and stare in another direction, pointing his ears forward to listen intently to some faint far sound. . . ."

Alertness combined with speed, handiness, and endurance makes Criollos good polo ponies. They also perform well in endurance competitions. In the 1930s, two Criollos, Mancha and Gato, accompanied an adventurous English schoolmaster named Aime Tschiffely on a 10,000-mile, two-year trek from the Argentine city of Buenos Aires to Washington, D.C.

Also bred from the horses of the pampas is the Chilean Horse, *el caballo chileno*. Resembling a small quarter horse, it has low withers, well-muscled forearms, and powerful hindquarters.

PATAGONIAN CRIOLLO

CABALLO CHILENO

43

ON THE FLAT

Polo

This fastest of all games originated in Tibet some 3,000 years ago and may have derived from the hunting of a marmotlike mammal. Every fall, men on horseback pursued the small animals and kept them from going into their burrows. In summertime, a ball replaced the animal and goals were substituted for burrows. *Polo* comes from the Tibetan word *pulu,* meaning "root" or "ball."

At first polo was an individual game with as many players as the field could accommodate. Women players sometimes rode donkeys with jeweled bridles and inlaid saddles. When the game spread east to China, the emperors of the T'ang Dynasty tapped their treasuries to buy fine ponies from beyond the Great Wall. Polo spread westward as far as Constantinople, and in time it became a team sport, with the number of players reduced to four. In India, polo was discovered by the British colonials and became immensely popular. By the 1880s, the game was being played in the United States.

Eight players, four to a team, attempt to drive a small four-ounce willow-root ball into the 8-yard space between their opponents' goal posts. Play is started when one of the two mounted umpires bowls the ball between the two teams lined up in the center of the 300-yard-long field. Then comes action!

Polo is a game of speed, beauty, and danger. Players ride off their opponents, and knock or hook their sticks. They risk injury from sticks, ball, ponies' heels, and falls. Ponies, too, collect kicks and sometimes fall. Standing in his stirrups, a player swings his mallet. His upper body moves independently of his seat and legs. The side of the mallet head hits the ball, driving it down the field toward the other team's goal posts. With sticks raised, the players charge after the ball, their lathered ponies' bandaged legs making a blur of color.

A player must not cross in front of an opponent who is pursuing the ball. Except for this right-of-way restriction, there are few rules. But when a player rides off another, maneuvering his pony so that it pushes the other pony away from the ball, the bumps are often hard. Or the player may hook an opponent's mallet. If he misuses his stick or obstructs right of way, the penalty may be a 60-yard or 40-yard free hit for the other team or a free hit from the foul site.

Shots are termed "near shots" when struck, backhand or forehand, on the left or near side of the pony; "off shots" when struck on the right or far side of the pony. The ball also is swung at under the pony's neck or belly or across its hindquarters.

Although teamwork is not apparent, it is important to a team's success. Positions in polo are flexible, and players cover for each other. Number 1 is the star goal scorer. Number 2 is a fast, aggressive player and a strong hitter. Number 3, often the team captain, excels in long drives and intercepts attacks. And Number 4, the back, guards the goal. Players are handicapped, with ratings of up to 10 goals. Their combined tally is the team's handicap, and if the team's rating is 19 or more, the game is high-goal polo.

Action on the polo field flows back and forth, interrupted only when a goal is scored, a foul is called, or the period ends. A game has four or five periods (or chukkers) of seven and a half minutes each. Between periods, the players dismount. Stirrups are run up on leathers, and girths are loosened to allow the ponies to blow. Then, with coolers thrown over their steaming bodies, the ponies are walked slowly in circles. Usually each player has several ponies, for no pony should play more than two periods.

A polo pony is actually a horse, 15 to 15.2 hands high. It must be well balanced and surefooted, for much of the game depends upon the polo pony and its ability to stop, turn, and gallop. Thoroughbred breeding predominates, and some ponies come off the track. Others are part Thoroughbred. Quarter horses often are used for indoor polo played in arenas much smaller than a polo field, with three players on a team and a soccer-type ball.

Agile, athletic, and responsive, a polo pony must be able to break into a gallop, to stop abruptly, rein back, or turn tightly on hocks or forehand. And it must be aggressive and fearless, ready to gallop at top speed into an opposing-team pony, sometimes at an angle sharp enough to knock the pony over, and able to endure bruising physical contact.

Above all, a polo pony must be intelligent, as was the small, flea-bitten gray with the neat polo tail that belonged to Team Captain Lutyens in Rudyard Kipling's *The Day's Work*. A homely Mongolian pony, the Maltese Cat proved himself after his rider suffered a broken collarbone. As the ponies took their places on the field, the Cat said: "And now, remember that this is the last quarter, and follow the ball. Back me up when I run, and follow the ball." Then the gallant little horse, guided only by his injured rider's legs, went into action and carried Lutyens and his team to victory.

Thoroughbreds and Racing

Beauty and function combine in the Thoroughbred. The head is small and refined, the neck long and graceful. The shoulders are well sloped and the chest is deep, with plenty of room for heart and lungs. The hindquarters are powerful, the hocks well let down, and the legs are clean and hard with tendons well defined. This conformation gives the Thoroughbred a long, free way of moving. With its courage, will to win, and ground-swallowing stride, the Thoroughbred is the fastest of all horse breeds, capable of running up to 40 miles per hour.

These aristocrats of the horse world trace their male lines of descent back to one of three foundation sires imported to England early in the eighteenth century: the Byerly Turk, the Darley Arabian, and the Godolphin Arabian, in fact a Barb. There were, of course, other stallions that influenced the breed, among them a gray, Alcock's Arabian, whose name is said to appear in the pedigree of every Thoroughbred that is a gray.

Race horses have been part of the English sporting scene since 1174 when the first recorded race took place at Smithfield. Horses that raced, most of them part Arabian, were called galloways or running horses. By the early 1700s, Arabian mares were being bred to stallions of known ancestry, and careful records were kept. A stud book was established, and in the 1821 issue the term *Thoroughbred* first appears.

In 1730 a horse named Bulle Rocke, a son of the Darley Arabian, was imported to Virginia. Among the horses imported after the Revolutionary War

were Diomed, a twenty-one-year-old who, in spite of his age, became the sire of many fast horses, and Messenger, whose blood influenced the development of the Standardbred as well as the Thoroughbred.

By 1860 racetracks were scattered throughout the East, the South, and the Midwest. After the Civil War, racing declined in the South but gained popularity in the North, where tracks opened at Saratoga in New York, Pimlico in Maryland, and Churchill Downs in Kentucky.

Among the legends of the early days of the American turf was Lexington, a thundering bay racer of the 1850s that broke the world's record for four miles and then raced against time to better his own record.

Man o' War, defeated only once—when he was left at the post—was so fast he never had to extend himself and always won with lengths to spare. Triple Crown winners (three-year-olds that have won the Kentucky Derby, the Preakness, and the Belmont) of recent years include the big strapping chestnut Secretariat and the bold brown Seattle Slew, whose three-race sweep was duplicated a year later by a flashing chestnut colt named Affirmed.

Geldings as well as stallions have left their mark in racing, from the small bay Seabiscuit to the mighty brown Forego. And now and then a filly shows exceptional speed, as did Ruffian, whose career as a three-year-old ended in tragedy when she broke a foreleg during a match race with the colt Foolish Pleasure.

Kentucky's famous bluegrass country with its large breeding farms is the home of many Thoroughbreds, although race horses today come from

Maryland, Virginia, California, Texas, Florida, New Jersey, and other states. All Thoroughbreds are registered by the Jockey Club and have their official birthday on January 1. Every Thoroughbred trained for the track has its registration number tattooed inside the upper lip to prevent a mix-up of identity or the substitution of a ringer, a fast horse in place of a slow horse.

The American Quarter Horse

From English Thoroughbreds imported to Virginia in the 1600s and bred to local horses of Andalusian ancestry came horses that showed agility, quickness, and speed over short distances. By 1665, the quarter running horse had become the original American race horse. Its fame as a short-distance runner spread quickly through the colonies. Much in demand as a stud was an English Thoroughbred named Janus, a winner of numerous four-mile races, imported in 1752. Although the Quarter Horse was not recognized as a breed until 1940, when the American Quarter Horse Society was founded, it is the earliest distinct type developed in America.

The first organized horse races in this country were held in Virginia on quarter-mile race paths. Over these straight dirt-road tracks the quarter running horses proved their speed, often in two-horse match races. Between races, the sturdy horses with powerful hindquarters and conspicuously developed muscles were used for farm work. In the early 1800s, replaced as a race horse by the Thoroughbred, the Quarter Horse went west with the settlers to plow the prairie sod and prove itself as a hard-working cow pony.

Short back, sturdy legs with low-set knees and hocks, low withers, a deep chest, and a broad, short head with foxlike ears are points of Quarter Horse conformation looked for by judges in halter classes. Trained as a cutting horse, the Quarter Horse must exhibit cow sense, as well as speed and agility to keep the steer, cow, or calf from rejoining the herd. For calf roping, the Quarter Horse has few rivals. From a standing start, it can reach top speed in three strides. It also possesses strength, ruggedness, and the power to stop the weight and drive of a steer. Some Quarter Horses show aptitude for jumping and make good hunters.

Quarter-horse racing is again popular. At tracks throughout the country, race meetings attract great crowds to see the quarter-milers cover 440 yards in less time (22 seconds) than the fastest Thoroughbred. The All-American Futurity at Ruidoso Downs, New Mexico, an event for two-year-olds, is the world's richest horse race. Its jackpot purse is a far cry from the sack of oats or round of whiskey that went to a match-race winner of years ago.

The majority of Quarter Horses, combining good looks and quiet manners, are pleasure horses.

The Morgan Horse

In 1795 Justin Morgan, a Vermont schoolteacher, acquired a two-year-old colt from Massachusetts. Figure matured into a small but sturdy horse, 14 hands high. Morgan used him for farm work, stump pulling, and timber hauling. All-around usefulness and a willing temperament soon made Figure much in demand as a stud.

While all Morgans are descended from Justin Morgan's small bay stallion, the breed has been refined by addition of Thoroughbred and saddlebred

MORGAN

blood. Compact in build, the Morgan has strong sloping shoulders and a deep-barreled chest. Its short limbs are slender, and its head has a slightly dished profile, wide-set large eyes, small ears set well apart, prominent jaws, and a well-chiseled muzzle. The Morgan's usefulness as an all-purpose horse is threatened by increasing emphasis on the show-ring type with long hoofs and animated way of going.

The Saddlebreds

The American Saddlebred was developed by settlers in Kentucky and other southern states who wanted an all-purpose, easy-gaited horse. The foundation sire was a Thoroughbred named Denmark. Tom Hal, a Canadian pacer that

THREE GAITED SADDLE HORSE

carried his physician-owner from Lexington to Louisville and back, a two-day round trip of some 160 miles, also influenced the breed. To improve type, Standardbred, Morgan, and other strains were introduced. The result was a strong, beautiful horse that offered a comfortable ride. During the Civil War, Confederate officers often were mounted on their own saddlers. General John Hunt Morgan's handsome stallion, Gaines Denmark, appears in the pedigrees of many saddle horses.

The saddle horse of the show ring is highly bred and trained. Alert and tense, it is seldom seen outside the ring. Hoofs are left as long as possible and weighted with special shoes to increase the horse's high action. Light chains or wooden rollers are sometimes fastened around pasterns during schooling sessions or when the horse is in its stall. The showy tail set is achieved by

FIVE GAITED SADDLE HORSE

WALK OF A 3 GAITED SADDLE HORSE

TROT OF THREE GAITED SADDLE HORSE

CANTER OF A THREE GAITED SADDLE HORSE

nicking (surgically cutting) the tail's depressor muscles and then using a tail-set harness so that the tail maintains this artificial position. Ginger, often applied under the tail just before the horse enters the ring, causes irritation that accentuates high carriage of the tail.

Refined and elegant, an American Saddlebred stands 15 to 16.1 hands high. Chestnut, bay, black, or gray, it is an eye-catcher and a crowd-pleaser. Its narrow, well-modeled head, with large, widely spaced eyes and long, mobile ears, is carried high. Its neck is long and gracefully arched. Shoulders are powerful and well sloped for smoothness of action. A short back and rounded barrel provide weight-carrying ability, while flat croup and rounded quarters give thrust to its gaits. The legs are long and clean. Saddlebreds are shown either as three-gaited, five-gaited, or fine harness horses.

The Three-gaited Saddle Horse, with clipped mane and pulled tail, sometimes is referred to as a "walk-trot horse." Three-gaiteds enter the ring at a flat-footed walk. Soon the call comes for them to trot. This most important gait is executed with even more exaggerated knee and hock action. The horses walk, canter, and walk again. Turning toward the ring fence, they reverse and repeat the same gaits. At all three gaits their action is collected and animated. Finally the horses line up in the center of the ring. Responding to the rider's raised hands and toe taps on the shoulder, each horse stretches or poses.

Three-gaited Saddle Horses are used for saddle-seat equitation. For these horses and their young riders, a high point of the year is the Good Hands event at the National Horse Show.

THE LAST JUDGMENT © BY KOEHL

WALK OF A FIVE GAITED SADDLE HORSE © BY NOSHI

TROT OF A FIVE GAITED SADDLE HORSE © BY NOSHI

SLOW GAIT

CANTER OF A FIVE GAITED SADDLE HORSE © BY NOSHI

Saddle-seat attire is a suit of matching color. The jacket is long and pleated; the jodhpurs, skin-tight over the knees, flare over ankle-high boots. Black, blue, gray, green, or brown suits often flash jacket linings that match the bright-colored ribbons used in the five-gaiteds' forelock and mane. Riders wear a derby or soft hat. Formal wear, for evening classes, consists of a dark-colored saddle suit, or a tuxedo-type jacket and top hat.

The five-gaited Saddle Horse enters the ring at a fast, animated trot, with hocks well under the body and head flexed at the poll. It is then shown at the walk, trot, slow gait, rack, and canter. Slow gait and rack, the two artificial gaits, require training. The slow gait is a syncopated four-beat running walk, performed with animated high action. When the call comes to "rack on," the hoofs strike the ground in rapid succession in four distinct beats. There is almost no vertical displacement of the horse's body. Speed and flashy action at the rack turn the judge's head and excite spectators who cheer their favorites around the ring. Thrilling to watch, the rack is smooth and fast, and tiring to the horse. Then, from a standstill along the ring fence, the horses break

into a canter. The high forward thrust of their forelegs makes it difficult to determine which lead the five-gaited is on. Again the horses walk and line up, usually head-to-tail down the center of the ring. The judge walks in and out down the line of posed horses, each a picture of alertness.

Some five-gaited horses are trained exclusively for Fine Harness competition. Other saddlers are shown in combination classes, first hitched to a four-wheeled buggy at the walk and trot, and then under saddle at a walk, trot, and canter.

The Tennessee Walking Horse

WALKING HORSE

Bred for use by plantation owners and their overseers, this horse was first called the plantation saddle horse. Its easy ambling walk and trot and straight-going canter made it ideal for riding up and down between long rows of crops. This use gave the walker its nickname, the turn-row.

A flashy big horse with a long and rather plain head, the Tennessee Walker is noted for its amiable disposition. A shorter, less arched neck, long shoulders, longer back with sloping croup and large-boned limbs distinguish it from the saddlebred.

Fifteen to 16 hands high, walkers come in all colors and often have splashy white markings. Their walk, with cadenced nodding of the head, is flat-footed. The running walk, a comfortable gliding gait that is inherited in the breed, covers ground at 6 to 9 miles per hour. In the show ring, the walker's speed nearly doubles. Each foot strikes the ground in a four-beat rhythm to produce a smooth rocking-chair gait that requires great strength of neck and shoulders and causes the vigorous head nodding which gives the walker another name, the nodder.

Not as high as the saddlebred's way of going, the walker's gait is free and extended, and it has enormous forward reach. Length of stride is such that the hind foot falls as much as 2 feet in front of the about-to-lift forefoot.

Walking horses excel as pleasure horses and as combination riding-and-driving horses. For the show ring, schooling and, unfortunately, the use of pain-inflicting devices increase the exaggerated high action and the overreaching of the hind feet at the running walk. Manes are long and tails flowing. Riders sit well back with long stirrups and hands held high. In Shelbyville, Tennessee, a week-long horse show, the Tennessee Walking Horse National Celebration, is held annually.

MOCHI

OVER FENCES

Hunters

> D'ye ken John Peel with his coat so gay?
> D'ye ken John Peel at the break of day?
> D'ye ken John Peel when he's far, far away,
> With his hounds and his horn in the morning?
>
> *From the hunting song "John Peel"*
> *by John Woodcock Graves*

Early on a fall morning the huntsman gathers his pack and moves on to cover, or wooded area, where the hounds, noses to ground and tails wagging, cast for scent. As the fox breaks cover, the huntsman sounds a series of single notes on his horn—"Gone away." The chase is on through fields and over stone walls and rail fences.

Runs often end in checks, when hounds lose the scent. Then the huntsman recasts the pack or lifts the hounds to another place. Once the hounds pick up the line, the chase resumes. Kills are infrequent. Usually the fox goes to ground (enters a den). Often criticized for their interest in a "blood sport," foxhunting enthusiasts are in fact the fox's benefactors. Their sport requires that large areas of open country be maintained and thus preserves habitat for foxes as well as other wild animals.

61

When a fox has gone to ground, the hounds are called off and the riders, after one by one thanking the MFH or master of foxhounds for the day's sport, turn away to hack home. In all likelihood the same fox will provide other days of exhilarating gallops and again test the hounds' ability to follow its line.

In days gone by a huntsman sometimes carried a Norwich or other small terrier. When the fox went to ground, the short-legged, wire-coated dog was set down. Scooting into the earth hole, the terrier badgered the fox until it emerged and was torn apart by the hounds.

Fox hunting came to North America with the British colonists. The sport became well established in Virginia and Maryland, with packs later being formed in New England, southern and midwestern states. Today there are some 146 hunts in the United States and Canada. The majority of the packs pursue live foxes. Some are "drag" hunts whose hounds trail a scent that is laid by dragging an anise-soaked bag over a predetermined route. In the West there are a few packs of hounds that chase coyotes instead of foxes.

Hunt meets occur from early fall until spring planting time, as often as two or three times a week. Horse shows, hunter trials, and race meetings occupy fox hunters during spring and summer. Then in late summer comes cubbing season, when young hounds are trained and green hunters are schooled.

A hunter is a type rather than a breed. Most hunters are Thoroughbreds or near-Thoroughbreds, big-striding, bold-going with size, speed, and jumping scope to keep up with hounds in open fields-and-fences country where scenting usually is good. But the type of hunter depends on a rider's weight (a lightweight hunter carries up to 165 pounds; a middleweight hunter carries between 165 and 185 pounds) and the country to be hunted. For hunting rough, boggy terrain, a horse with some pony blood is useful. A half- or three-quarter-bred makes a fine heavyweight hunter (up to carrying more than 185 pounds). Irish hunters, famed for their ability to leap banks and ditches, originally were bred from draft mares.

A show hunter or a field hunter should have good bone and be well proportioned, with shoulders that slope and with back, loins, and hindquarters that indicate power. It must move well, free and straight at the walk and trot, and have a long, low, effortless galloping stride. Last but by no means least in importance are manners. A horse that pulls, fusses, refuses to wait its turn at a panel, plays the fool by bucking, bolts, kicks at another horse or, worst of all, at the hounds does not make a pleasant ride in the hunt field.

A hunter competing in a Corinthian or Appointments class takes a post-and-rail fence in fine form. Its rider wears formal hunting attire, a shadbelly coat and silk hunting hat, and carries a hunting whip with thong. In this event the horse's performance and way of going over the hunt course will count 85 percent, while the rider's dress (livery of the hunt to which she belongs) and appointments (a pair of string gloves tucked under the billets of the saddle, a sandwich case that contains a chicken or ham sandwich, and a flask filled with port wine) make up 15 percent of the judge's score. Not only do judges check each of these items, but on occasion they sample a sandwich or tipple a flask.

In the show ring, hunters are separated into two groups. Working hunters are judged on performance and fitness, while conformation hunters are scored on their looks as well as their performance. Fences simulate the types of obstacles found in the hunt field: brush, post-and-rail, snake fences, in-and-outs, stone walls, and chicken coops (wooden A-frames used to panel wire fencing in hunt country).

Pairs of hunters, matched in color and size, must maintain a good hunting pace and jump abreast or sometimes tandem. Hunt teams, each representing a different hunt, usually perform tandem, keeping an even, safe hunting distance between the three horses.

Junior hunters are shown by riders under eighteen years old. Most of these young riders also compete in hunt-seat equitation classes. Some of them qualify, by winning a certain number of blue ribbons during the year, to compete for the Championship Trophy of the American Society for Prevention of Cruelty to Animals at the National Horse Show. Better known as the Maclay Trophy, this plate is engraved with the names of many United States Equestrian Team members who were top junior riders in their day.

Jumpers

Jumping is essentially an extension of the horse's normal stride. Approach is the all-important preparation for a jump. Riders rate their horses, counting the

CORINTHIAN   HUNTER   CUT BY MOCHI

number of strides between closely spaced obstacles, lengthening or shortening them as necessary. The fences may be 5 to 6 feet high, with spreads of up to 6 feet. Pace of approach and number of strides determine whether a horse, like this jumper handily clearing the triple bar, makes an effortless clean jump, or "piles up the timber."

Jumpers may be any kind of horse. Hackneys have produced top jumpers, and now and then a saddlebred shows talent over fences. Some jumpers are big, powerful, even cumbersome-looking horses that have come from work on a farm or life in a hack stable. Others are athletic Thoroughbreds. In the schooling area, before a jumper class, they pop back and forth over a 5-foot fence, needing only a stride or two before take-off. A jumper that becomes careless may receive a light rap from a hand-held pole as it goes over the fence. This practice, called poling, causes a jumper to tuck up its forefeet and hind feet.

Jumper scoring follows rules of the American Horse Shows Association. Jumping style does not count. Only jumping faults and, in some events, elapsed time are scored. In case of a jumping tie, the fences are raised and a jump-off decides the winner.

Show Jumping and Eventing

During the 1940s when Ugo Mochi attended the National Horse Show at Madison Square Garden, international competition took place between military teams from Italy, Ireland, Britain, Canada, Chile, Mexico, and the United States. Whether it was a big, bold Irish jumper or a small, agile Mexican-team horse in the ring, excitement ran high during an international jumping class. Refusals, knockdowns, falls of rider and sometimes of horse, were added thrills for spectators.

Many of the military horse-and-rider combinations also competed in the Olympics. Among them was the United States Team's Democrat, negotiating a Liverpool jump during the 1948 Olympics in London, with Colonel F. F. Wing up.

In 1949 the horse cavalry was disbanded. France, Canada, and Mexico

sent teams to the Garden that fall, but there was no U.S. Army Team to compete. Concerned horsemen set out to form and fund their own team for international competition. Thus the USET (United States Equestrian Team), now one of the most important equestrian organizations in the world, was formed.

The USET competes in the Olympics (held every four years), in the Pan American Games (held in the year before the Olympics), and in the World Championships (held midway between the Olympic Games). For each of these international events the USET picks a dressage team and a combined training team as well as a show-jumping team to represent the United States.

In show jumping, distances between fences are critical. This is why riders first walk a course, analyzing the number of strides (a horse's strong-cantering stride averages about 10 feet) between fences and the distances in combinations. A demanding course of ten to twelve or more fences is made up of oxers with 4-foot spreads, rails set at 5 feet or higher, a solid-looking wall, gates, a brush, and sometimes a bank jump or a water jump.

Speed classes, or "riding against the clock," test a jumper's handiness. Riders attempt to save time by turning or "playing angles," for time is lost when speed is excessive and turns are loose. Usually the winner is a horse that is cleverly ridden at a smooth, even pace with economical turns.

Time does not count in puissance classes, open to both international team members and competitors from the jumper division. *Puissance* is a French word meaning "strength." Puissance horses must have talent and strength to jump the enormous obstacles. Rarely do they use more than three or four driving strides before take-off. These strides and finding the right take-off spot are critical. Take-off comes from a strong, hock-gathering stride 5 or 6 feet from the jump. If several horses have no-fault rounds, jump-offs take place, each time over a shortened course. Finally only two fences remain, one a big spread, the other a towering wall that may be set at 7 feet. Then the take-off appears to be almost at the base of the wall, and the horse, with exaggerated bascule (curve of body as forequarters counterbalance hindquarters in seesaw effect), curls over the top.

The FEI (Federation Equestre Internationale) governs international show jumping and dictates clear-cut penalties: four faults for each fence knocked

down, three for the first refusal, six for the second, and elimination for the third.

Combined training or eventing is a rigorous equestrian discipline. For three, four, five, or more years, horse and rider work together to achieve the peak of training fitness required to compete in a Three-Day Event.

The first-day dressage phase is a test of the horse's obedience and precision, as well as its suppleness and responsiveness as the rider guides it through a series of prescribed exercises.

On the second day, horse and rider face a test of speed and endurance. Two phases of roads and tracks, or work on the flat, are separated by a steeplechase phase over fences. Then—after a ten-minute compulsory halt and vet check, when the veterinarian looks for a drop in pulse rate as an indication of whether a horse is able to continue—comes the fourth and final cross-country phase. Over a 4- or 5-mile course, uphill and down, the courage of horse and rider is challenged by some thirty formidable obstacles—banks, brooks, slides, drops, vertical rails, spreads, and open ditches. An event horse must have great confidence in its rider and be bold and clever to face these large, solid jumps and negotiate them at speed (an average speed of 21 miles per hour must be maintained in cross-country).

Stadium jumping takes place on the third day. Horse and rider compete over a moderately difficult course of ten or twelve knockdown, show-ring fences, a test of their fitness and readiness to go again the day after the grueling cross-country phase. When each competitor's marks for the three tests are added, the lowest penalty scores determine the winning horse-and-rider teams.

FINE HARNESS HORSE

THE FINE HARNESS HORSE

This division is restricted to Five-gaited Saddle Horses. Wearing light show harnesses and snaffle bits, the horses enter the ring one at a time. Their drivers, in evening attire if the occasion demands, sit erect in small four-wheeled road wagons as the horses circle the ring, first at a showy park gait, then a trot, a walk, and an animated walk. As a test of manners, the horses must stand quietly, posed and stretched, after lining up in the center of the ring.

During the 1940s Parading Lady, owned and driven by Josephine Abercrombie, took many blue ribbons in this division.

THE ROADSTER

The Roadster or Light Harness division is open to horses (or ponies) of most any breed. This Roadster, a 15.3-hand chestnut gelding, fulfills requirements of height (horses shown as Roadsters must stand between 15.1 and 16 hands) and color (which must be solid). Like most Roadsters, he is a well-built horse, with a natural tail and flowing mane and a forelock that has been clipped. Unlike most roadsters, he moves with high action.

Harnessed to a road wagon or "bike" and always shown in a light bit, Roadsters enter the ring clockwise at a jog. When they reverse direction, their drivers ask for a road gait and show their horses at speed. Speed at the trot is a Roadster's most outstanding attribute. Even when they are shown under saddle, the judge looks for a very fast, ground-covering trot. And a Roadster must demonstrate good manners.

THE HEAVY HARNESS HORSE

The Hackney Horse, properly shown in this division, is seldom seen today. A high-stepping, elegant harness horse, the Hackney was developed in England as roads improved and the need arose for a lighter and faster type of horse. A direct ancestor was the Norfolk trotter, a light horse of mostly Thoroughbred and Arabian blood. The word *hackney* is said to come from the French *haquenée,* which means "ambling horse." Later on the term *hack,* derived from *hackney,* was used to designate a carriage horse for common hire. Often a hack horse's life was that of a drudge.

Robust-bodied and handsome, Hackneys may stand up to 16 hands, although most of them are about 15.2 hands high. Bay, dark brown, sometimes black or chestnut, they have a brilliant and animated way of going at the trot. Driven singly or in pairs, Hackney Horses dominated the carriage shows of a century ago. On the streets a matched pair of Hackneys was an object of much admiration. Occasionally Hackneys were driven tandem, one in front of the other, or three Hackneys were hitched, a pair in the wheel position and one out front on its own. With no shafts to restrain it, this lead Hackney had to be steady-going. Otherwise a bad shy would cause it to turn completely around and face the wheel pair. Hackney Horses also were used as four-in-hands (two pairs, one in front of the other) to pull road coaches. When a woman drove, the Hackney Horse usually was harnessed to a light carriage called a phaeton.

In the show ring, a viceroy with bicycle tires was used for Hackneys. This pair, slowing from a park gait to a smart trot, demonstrates the small head, long and rather thickset neck, low withers, compact but not-too-deep body, and high tail set that are Hackney characteristics. Their shoulder action is free, and their forelegs are thrown forward as well as up, with a brief moment of hesitation at the height of each step. When they halt, with forelegs straight and hind legs stretched, the pair will stand heads high and ears pricked. Hackneys always appear alert.

Heavy harness Hackneys were imported in large numbers during the 1870s and 1880s, while in England small Hackneys were being bred selectively. Then, in 1883, A. J. Cassatt of Philadelphia, president of the American Hackney Horse Society, showed a pony-size import, Little Wonder, creating a sensation at Madison Square Garden in New York City.

THE HACKNEY PONY

As the popularity of the larger horses declined, the number of Hackney Ponies increased. At first the top winners at shows were imported ponies. Among them was King of the Plain, a star performer during the 1930s and the sire of Highland Cora and King of the Highlands, ponies that influenced nearly every Hackney pedigree.

Pony character is evident in these small versions of the Hackney Horse. Prominent eyes, small pricked ears, and an always alert expression are characteristic. So is a well-defined crest of the neck, accentuated when the

head is tucked in. Sturdy chest, sloping shoulders, well-sprung ribs, and squarish, muscular hindquarters are also typical of these ponies, 12 to 14 hands high.

Hours of training, proper shoeing, grooming the bay or brown coat until it gleams, braiding the fourteen tight little braids, brushing the 6-inch nubbin of a docked tail, cleaning harness, and polishing the viceroy ready the Hackney Pony for the show ring. Driving skill is needed to produce the balance and rhythm of a brilliant performance. With extravagant action, knees are raised high and hoofs flung forward; hocks come up almost to touch the body.

For evening classes at the National Horse Show, Dr. Elise Strang L'Esperance wore evening dress and hat to drive her Hackney Pony pair, Sir Richard Hi and Mad Acres Mischief. Ugo Mochi found many of his horse and pony models at Dr. L'Esperance's Red Blinds Stable, located near his home. And from her box at the horse show in Madison Square Garden, he had a ringside view of horses and events. This winning pair demonstrates near-perfect cadence of hoof-fall, something judges look for when Hackneys are harnessed as a pair or in tandem. When the ponies lined up, a "header" entered the ring to stand in front of each pair.

COACHES AND CARRIAGES

A coach, by definition, has four wheels, springs, and a roof, while a carriage is an open vehicle. Spring carriages became popular in Europe during the sixteenth century when various types appeared, each suited to a purpose. Springing or suspending the carriage body with chains or leather straps from curved chassis supports as well as improved roads made traveling a more pleasant experience. As an artist, Ugo Mochi was fascinated by the craft of coaches and carriages.

One of the earliest coaches was the fiacre, first used to take visitors to the sanctuary of Saint-Fiacre de Bris, 25 miles from Paris. This spring-type coach, with smaller front wheels for greater mobility, plied the route from Paris to the shrine and back with such frequency that eventually the road was named for the saint. In time the fiacre, equipped with distance-recording meter, became the first taxi. There were always one or more of the small coaches ready for hire outside the Hotel Saint-Fiacre in Paris where Ugo Mochi often stayed.

SECOND STATE COACH BY FERRI FOR CARDINAL RINALDO D'ESTE MAGNIFICENT ENTRANCE IN ROME 1688

Rome in the eighteenth century was a city of splendid coaches and carriages. Many coaches, including this one used by Cardinal Rinaldo d'Este, were ornately decorated and gilded.

On state occasions, royal carriages often were driven by one or more mounted postilions, who guided the wheel and lead horses while the footman and groom stood behind. But royalty also enjoyed the use of simpler carriages.

The sultan of Turkey was fond of outings in a two-wheeled cart pulled by four matched ponies.

During the nineteenth century, many types of horse-drawn vehicles rolled along city streets and jounced over country roads. With her Irish wolfhound coursing alongside, this lady drives her fast-stepping harness ponies to an Irish

carrick. The spider phaeton was a fashionable carriage for the wealthy. A footman sat behind the driver on a skeleton rumbleseat. For getting about in town or over country roads, nothing was handier than a gig.

HORSES BRED FOR HARNESS

As carriage makers in England, France, Germany, and later on in the United States turned out a seemingly endless array of smart and light vehicles, various kinds of coach and carriage horses were being bred. Some, like the harness Percheron, were bred to pull heavy coaches. Others, intended for lighter coaches and carriages, were bred for looks as well as speed, or for a stylish way of going.

The Cleveland Bay, a Yorkshire breed developed from pack animals during the sixteenth century and later refined by addition of Thoroughbred blood, is noted for its stamina, substance, style, and handsome bright bay color. Except for a small star, it has no other white markings. Eye-catching as a matched pair or a four-in-hand, the Cleveland Bay is also a natural jumper and a weight carrier. It is often crossed with the Thoroughbred to produce a sturdy field hunter.

ANGLO NORMAN

OLDENBURG COACH HORSE

HANOVERIAN

The Anglo-Norman was developed in the 1830s when Thoroughbred stallions were crossed with Norman mares descended from the powerful war horses of the William the Conqueror's time. It was used as a carriage horse for the well-to-do. A big (16.2 hands high) horse with a heavy body that sometimes appears out of harmony with its light-boned limbs, the Anglo-Norman was also used as a saddle horse.

The typical Oldenburg coach horse was a deep-chested, heavy animal with a massive neck, a short stout back, and an immense croup. As need for such a horse declined, the breed was refined by introducing Thoroughbred, Hanoverian, and Cleveland Bay blood.

Characteristically mild-mannered and willing, Oldenburgs today appear as matched teams, often grays, at driving events. They also compete in show jumping and dressage. Only a slightly lumbering canter betrays their heritage of farm horse, charger, and coach horse.

The Hanoverian was one of three types of cavalry horses developed during the seventeenth and eighteenth centuries. George I, king of England from 1714 to 1727, and subsequent reigning Hanoverian kings, all of them named George, took great interest in the development of this breed of German riding and driving horse. George II founded the stud at Celle, where Hanoverians are still bred today. The foundation sires at Celle were fourteen black Holsteins. Trakehner and Norman stallions and, most important, English Thoroughbreds sent by the Hanoverian kings were used in later crosses.

Typically large-bodied and long-legged, the Hanoverian has a well-arched neck and high withers and rump. Whatever its color, it usually has white markings on the head and lower legs. The Hanoverian's energetic trot, smooth, rhythmic canter, and mild disposition combine to make it a good dressage horse. Powerful build, strong back and legs, and well-muscled shoulders and hindquarters provide the drive that also makes it a fine show jumper.

A handsome horse, usually brown and often with white on its lower legs, the Holstein orginally was bred as a coach horse in the Elbe River district of Germany. The breed became popular in France during the sixteenth, seventeenth, and eighteenth centuries. In those days it was a big, strong horse with rather high action, noble-looking in spite of its convex-shaped head.

Today the Holstein carries Thoroughbred and Cleveland Bay blood. Well-matched Holstein teams compete in driving events. The breed also has produced outstanding show jumpers, horses that excel in precision of style rather than speed over a course.

In 1732 Frederick William I, king of Prussia, established a stud at Trakehnen where light, elegant, spirited horses were bred for the royal stables. Some 200 years of selective breeding have transformed and perfected the Trakehner from a small native farm horse to the handsome horse of today, the finest of the German breeds.

Much like the Thoroughbred in conformation, the Trakehner is long-legged and light-boned. With a reputation for being high-strung and even temperamental, it is a fast horse and a superb jumper.

Named for the small town of Lipizza where a stud farm was founded in the 1580s to breed harness and riding horses, the Lipizzan is the remarkable horse of the Spanish Riding School in Vienna. Almost always gray—so gray they appear white—Lipizzans have long bodies, strong hindquarters, and well-boned limbs.

LIPIZZAN

TROTTING HORSES

Fast and flashy road horses, often called roadsters, were prized by their owners during the 1800s. Pulling abreast, the owner of one speedy trotter challenged another. Then their trotting horses opened up. Such contests on country roads were called brushes. In New York City, the then-fashionable street called the Bowery was a favorite site for these chance encounters, which caused pedestrians as well as carriage drivers to protest for their safety. Some years later the contests moved to Third Avenue, laid out as a wide trotting stretch. By 1840, there were a few tracks, and trotting horses were harnessed to light, high-wheeled sulkies with barely enough room for a driver to perch, legs extended and feet in shaft stirrups on either side of the horse's hindquarters. It was only a matter of years before an American breed of trotting horse, the Standardbred, developed.

American trotting stock has influenced harness racing in Italy, France, and Germany. Russia has a trotting breed of its own called the Orlov.

THE STANDARDBRED

In 1788 an eight-year-old gray English Thoroughbred stallion named Messenger arrived in Philadelphia. Undistinguished as a race horse, this import sired many fast-trotting horses and became the foundation sire of the Standardbred. A great-grandson, William Rysdyk's Hambletonian, foaled in 1849, not only showed exceptional speed but influenced the breed by siring more than 1,300 foals. Nearly all Standardbreds trace back to Rysdyk's Hambletonian. A famous harness race, the Hambletonian, is named for this bay horse.

When the American Trotting Register was formed in 1871, a requirement for registration was that a horse trot or pace the mile in standard time (2:30 minutes for a trotter and 2:25 minutes for a pacer). Thus did the Standardbred acquire its name. Today the standard is 2:20, and to race in a recognized event a harness horse must be able to trot or pace the mile within this time limit.

Selective breeding of Standardbreds has resulted in ever-faster times. For twenty-eight years a trotting record for the mile in 1:55¼ set in 1938 by the famous 16.1-hand gray gelding Greyhound stood firm. And there was Dan Patch, the celebrated pacer whose 1906 record for the mile in 1:55 was never recognized. Today's top trotters go the mile in 1:55 and several tenths of a second, while top time for a pacer is 1:52. Harness racing enthusiasts throng nightly to New York's Roosevelt and Yonkers raceways, where the fastest Standardbreds flash around the huge floodlit ovals.

Longer-bodied, shorter-legged, and heavier-boned than a Thoroughbred, the Standardbred has a coarser head with straight or slightly convex profile. Its ears are long, and when it races, its elastic nostrils flare wide to take in more air. Its neck is relatively short and straight. The fine-haired mane, usually clipped over the poll, is long and straight; the tail is thick and long. Often a Standardbred's hips appear higher than its withers, a conformation feature that gives trotting pitch. The position of the hind legs behind, rather than under the croup, provides the pistonlike driving action of a trotter or pacer at top speed. Standardbreds range from 15 to 16 hands high; a few of them stand taller. Many are bays; some are brown, chestnut, or black. Occasionally a Standardbred is gray.

Pacing, a tendency inherited by some Standardbreds, is derived from a roadster-type horse known as the Narragansett pacer. Because they move with lateral (instead of diagonal) leg pairs, pacers are sometimes called sidewheelers. Front and hind legs on the same side move forward together in this awkward-looking two-beat gait, which is actually faster (about one percent) than its diagonal counterpart. The tendency to pace shows up among Standardbred foals at play in the pasture.

There are famous Standardbred breeding establishments, such as Castleton Farm in Kentucky and Hanover Shoe Farms in Pennsylvania. But many harness horses are foaled on small farms that have only a few broodmares. January 1 is every Standardbred's birthday, regardless of foaling date. As two-year-olds they start training as trotters or pacers. Once accustomed to the harness, the young horses are trained by line driving, a driver walking behind them. Then they are hitched to a jogging cart. Finally they are harnessed to a 30-pound sulky with a low seat, small wheels, and bicycle tires. In every workout, the most important lesson is always to trot or pace at top speed and never to gallop. A leg harness, or hopples, is used on most pacers to prevent their breaking stride. Often a trotter wears knee boots, held in place by a suspender strap over the shoulders, for protection. Felt ankle and shin boots and rubber bell boots and strikes are used to prevent injury from overreaching hind hoofs.

When race day comes, each horse has 4 or 5 miles of warming up, with in-between cooling-out sessions, before it goes to post. Except at Grand Circuit events such as the Hambletonian, where the best of three heats determines the winner, harness races are single contests. The thrill comes when the trotters or pacers move into action behind the foldaway starting gate mounted on top of the starter's car. Almost as important as the horse's speed is the driver's skill in knowing just when to ask his horse to move ahead and in guiding horse and sulky in tight company.

Although most drivers are professionals, many of them (unlike the jockeys who ride Thoroughbreds) are also the trainers of the horses they drive, and sometimes even the owners. Gentle and cooperative by nature, trotting horses since the time of Rysdyk's Hambletonian have enjoyed close association with their owners.

Standardbreds also race at state and county fairs, where their drivers are often amateurs. And they compete at horse shows in roadster classes. When its driver "turns it on," the Standardbred responds with long, flashing strides. Then it slows again, when the call comes to "jog them down."

THE ORLOV

When Count Aleksey Grigoryevich Orlov retired from military service in 1774, at the end of the Russo-Turkish War, he turned to breeding horses. Hoping to produce a fast, strong trotter suitable for driving singly or in a troika (team of three horses abreast), he obtained an Arabian stallion named Smetanka from the sultan of Turkey. Smetanka was bred to mares of several breeds. In 1784 a grandson of Smetanka was foaled. The colt matured into a long-legged stallion, with hindquarters noticeably higher than his withers. The dapple-gray Barss (or Bars I) showed exceptional speed at the trot and frequently was driven to a sleigh by Count Orlov himself. Barss became the foundation sire of the Orlov breed.

A small Arablike head, wide chest, and long back are characteristic of the usually gray Orlov, a horse that is a slightly smaller, more lightly built, and longer-legged version of the Standardbred. Although not as fast as the American trotter (top time for the mile by an Orlov is 2:06 as compared with 1:56, a good time for a Standardbred), the Orlov shows greater endurance over distances of several miles.

Harness racing became popular in nineteenth-century Russia, and there were many Orlov stud farms. The handsome grays also trotted along city streets, harnessed to fine carriages in the summer and to sleighs and troikas during the long, cold winter.

Many of the pony breeds derive from an ancient pony type related to the tarpan that once ranged over Iceland, Ireland, the Hebrides, and the Faroe Islands. Sturdy and short-legged, this Celtic pony probably looked much like the Norwegian Dun or Fjord pony of today.

Always dun, the Fjord pony has black points and a black stripe that runs from forelock through its light-colored mane (usually clipped to a 4- or 5-inch upright length to show the stripe), and along its spine to disappear among the black hairs of its thick tail. Strong, hardy, and sure-footed, these chunky 14- to 14.2-hand ponies have a seemingly tireless, shuffling trot that makes them ideal cart ponies. They are also used for riding and as pack ponies in the fjord country of Norway.

Hardiness and endurance characterize the Mongolian pony, whose nomad owners have ridden the steppes for centuries. Many of their ponies are domesticated. Others are semi-wild and once interbred with Przewalski horses. This medium-size (12.2 to 13.3 hands high) pony has a heavy head, thick neck and shoulders, and a deep chest. Its mane is long and scraggly, and its tail sweeps the ground. Its tough hoofs are worn by the rocky soil.

Closely related to the Mongolian pony is the Sining pony, bred and raised on mountain pastures in northwestern China and used for pack work. An ancient caravan route to Tibet passes through Sining (or Hsi-ning), the capital city of Tsinghai province, and over it for centuries the ponies have trekked, heavily laden with wool, hides, salt, and timber for trade.

Ponies, generally thought of as animals for children to ride, are intelligent and quick to learn, wrong as well as right. They are mischievous and sometimes obstinate. Small ponies, particularly Shetlands, that have earned a reputation for being stubborn and tricky are usually too small for an adult to ride and clever enough to know they are stronger than a child. While some ponies are too much for their young riders to handle, most of them provide fun and are the best of companions for pony trekking, pony clubbing, gymkhanas, and just backyard fun.

From the smallest of the pony-ride ponies to the fine pony hunters in the show ring, ponies have a charm of their own. Perhaps their individualism stems from a rugged heritage of subsisting on moors and mountain slopes, for each of the pony breeds is a hardy type, well adapted to its own environment.

THE WELSH PONY

Centuries ago, during a royal visit, the king of England was so infuriated by the sight of stunted, scruffy ponies grazing the rough hills and boggy moors of northern Wales that he ordered them destroyed. But the mountain ponies were wily, and many escaped slaughter. Today in parts of Wales their descendants pull carts and plows and carry farmers to tend their sheep.

Because of their small size, Welsh ponies were used in the mines, often spending all their lives underground, hauling heavy coal carts along dark, narrow, low-ceilinged tunnels. In the early 1800s, an English Thoroughbred named Merlin, one of the fastest race horses of his time, was retired and turned out for a life of ease on the Welsh hillsides. Merlin consorted with the ponies and proved such a successful sire that the local Welsh people began to call the ponies "merlins." Arabian and Hackney as well as Thoroughbred blood influence the Welsh pony. The Arabian influence is apparent in the typical Welsh pony head, its often gray color, the way it carries its tail, and its action.

85

The Welsh pony is an attractive animal. Its head is small and well chiseled, with a tapered muzzle and large, prominent eyes that are widely spaced and low set. Its small ears are sharply pointed. Its neck is long and well arched, crested in a stallion. Sloping shoulders and strong, short-coupled body make it a fine mover with quick free action, and a bold jumper. A tail that is well set-on adds a flourish to this mannerly pony's way of going.

Cross-bred ponies—Welsh-Thoroughbred and Welsh-Arabian—make fine small hunters for older children who are competent riders.

THE DARTMOOR PONY

For centuries, rugged ponies have lived on the bleak, wind-swept moorlands of southwest England, where they graze beneath mist-shrouded tors. Their long forelocks and bushy manes and tails protect them from wind and cold, and their shaggy coats shed rain as well as any oilskin.

Every fall these Dartmoor ponies are rounded up and new foals are branded or sold. Another annual event is the Dartmoor Society Pony Show. Small in size (12.2 hands) and placid in disposition, Dartmoors are considered ideal ponies for very young riders.

The purebred Dartmoor is dark in color (bay, brown, or black) and has no white markings. It has small, sharply pointed ears, a well-crested neck, a short back, well-muscled hindquarters, and stocky legs.

THE EXMOOR PONY

"Ponies on the moor, I always wanted to paint them . . ." wrote Sir Alfred J. Munnings, a sporting artist. "Wild ponies wandering free over thousands of acres of wide, undulating expanse. Herds of twenty or thirty, using their own territories—keeping to them, as birds do. If you want to find them, they have vanished. When least expecting them they appear on a skyline, or far below in a sheltered combe." The ponies Munnings longed to paint were Exmoors.

Exmoor ponies are brown with mealy-colored muzzles and eye rings and never any white markings. They have run wild on the high moors that stretch between Devon and Somerset for longer than any other ponies in Britain. Originally they were used as pack ponies. Today these small ponies (11.1 to 12.3 hands high) with thick manes and tails are prized as mounts for small children.

"Every child who saw me used to say: 'Oh! I wish I had a pony just like that!'" Thus did Mousie, a brown pony with a mealy nose, introduce himself in Golden Gorse's tale *Moorland Mousie.* Describing his foaling place, Withypool Common, Mousie continued: "There were several herds of ponies, twelve or more in each herd. These ponies on the hill-side—bays, light brown and dark browns, occasionally a chestnut—made vivid splashes of colour. All were busy grazing; it is hard to pick up a living on Exmoor, and of animals cared for by man, only the sheep and the ponies can do it."

THE NEW FOREST PONY

The New Forest, for nearly nine centuries the hunting preserve of Saxon kings, extends across 100 square miles of lower Hampshire in England. Here and there, roads wind among venerable trees, but much of the New Forest is bare of trees. Among the creatures of the open expanses of heath are the ponies, whose winding trails, trampled firm by countless hoofs, lead up slope and down through heather and around clusters of yellow furze. For browsing on such prickly vegetation, the New Forest pony has a protective moustache on its upper lip.

Some 1,500 ponies run free through the New Forest. Occasionally they wander into villages and graze in yards. Every fall, pony drifts are held. Herds are driven into large pens. Foals are branded, some of the mares and young ponies are sold, and stallions are removed to their owners' stables until the following spring. The New Forest Pony Breeding and Cattle Society's show is a springtime event.

Hardy, sure-footed, and well built, the New Forest pony is of medium size (about 13.3 hands high) and usually brown or bay. It has a well-set head with rather long ears, a short neck but shoulders that are well sloped, a deep chest,

short back, strong legs, and a low-set tail. Like the other moorland ponies, New Forests are known for their good temperament.

THE CONNEMARA PONY

Centuries of running free over rocky slopes and crags and across fields edged by stone walls in the Connemara mountain district of County Galway in western Ireland developed the Connemara pony breed. Each year, before the Connemara Pony Show at Clifden, the ponies are driven into boggy areas where they are easily captured with ropes over their necks and quickly gentled. Within a day's time, farmers are seen bicycling along the roads with their newly caught Connemara trotting behind on a loose shank.

The Connemara is a sensible, rugged pony and a superb jumper. Soundness and good temperament are also characteristic of these handsome ponies, 13 to 14.2 hands high. Connemaras have good bone, well-sloped shoulders, and powerful hindquarters. They carry their young riders in the hunt field and take part in pony club activities, and a few of them go on to the level of Three-Day Combined Training events. Connemaras that exceed the pony limit of 14.2 hands often are the favorite field hunters of lightweight adults.

Ponies and horses—bred for riding and bred for harness, bred to run and bred to trot, the steppe-grazers and the mustangs, armor-carrying war horse and swift battle steed—all have played their parts in human history. As childhood companions, faithful hunters and bold jumpers, pleasure horses, race horses and harness horses, and handy polo ponies, their ongoing roles are assured.